Pioneers of Earth Science

Lynn Van Gorp, M.S.

Earth and Space Science Readers:
Pioneers of Earth Science

Publishing Credits

Editorial Director
Dona Herweck Rice

Associate Editor
Joshua BishopRoby

Editor-in-Chief
Sharon Coan, M.S.Ed.

Creative Director
Lee Aucoin

Illustration Manager
Timothy J. Bradley

Publisher
Rachelle Cracchiolo, M.S.Ed.

Science Contributor
Sally Ride Science

Science Consultants
Nancy McKeown,
Planetary Geologist
William B. Rice,
Engineering Geologist

Teacher Created Materials
5301 Oceanus Drive
Huntington Beach, CA 92649-1030
http://www.tcmpub.com

ISBN 978-0-7439-0558-9

Printed in Malaysia
THU001.48806

Table of Contents

Maps and Globes 4

Making the Way 8

Changing the Map 18

Protecting Nature's Beauty 22

Geologist: Diane Evans 26

Appendices 28

- Lab: Earth Movement 28
- Glossary 30
- Index 31
- Sally Ride Science 32
- Image Credits 32

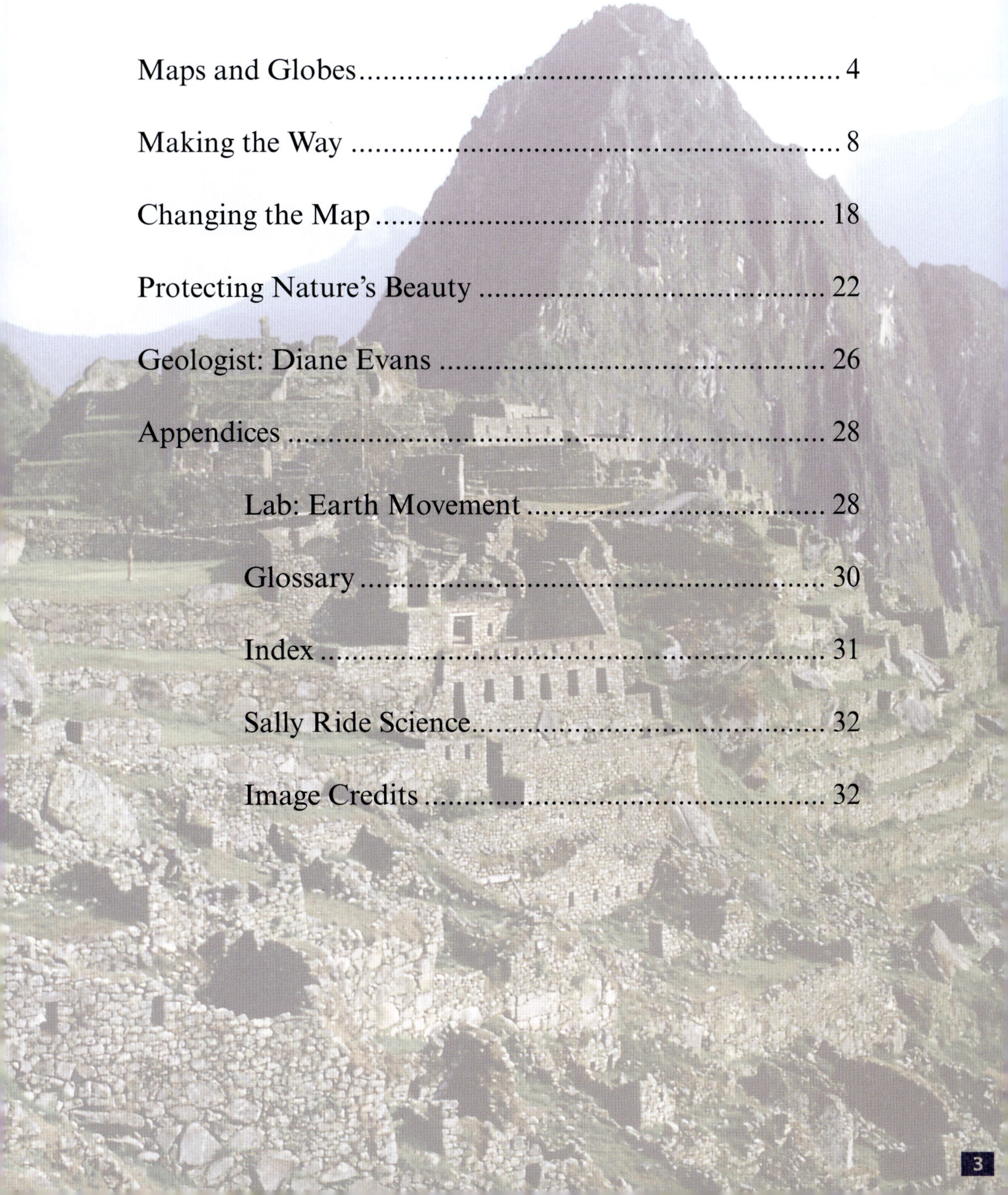

Maps and Globes

Mapmaking is an art form. The first maps were made thousands of years ago. Maps are one of the best ways for people to know the land. They are very important to scientists who study the earth.

Gerardus Mercator is one of the best known mapmakers of all time. He was born in 1512, in Belgium. He was interested in **geography**.

Gerardus Mercator

Although Mercator was an engraver of brass plates, he found a way to use his interest in geography to make a living. He worked with two other men to make a **globe**. He then worked alone to make a map of Palestine and then one of the world. They were called **map projections.** The world map showed the globe spread out to a flat surface.

There is one problem with a Mercator projection map. The size and shape of the land near the poles is not correct. Europe and North America look much bigger than Africa. In fact, Africa is much bigger than both of them!

an early projection map

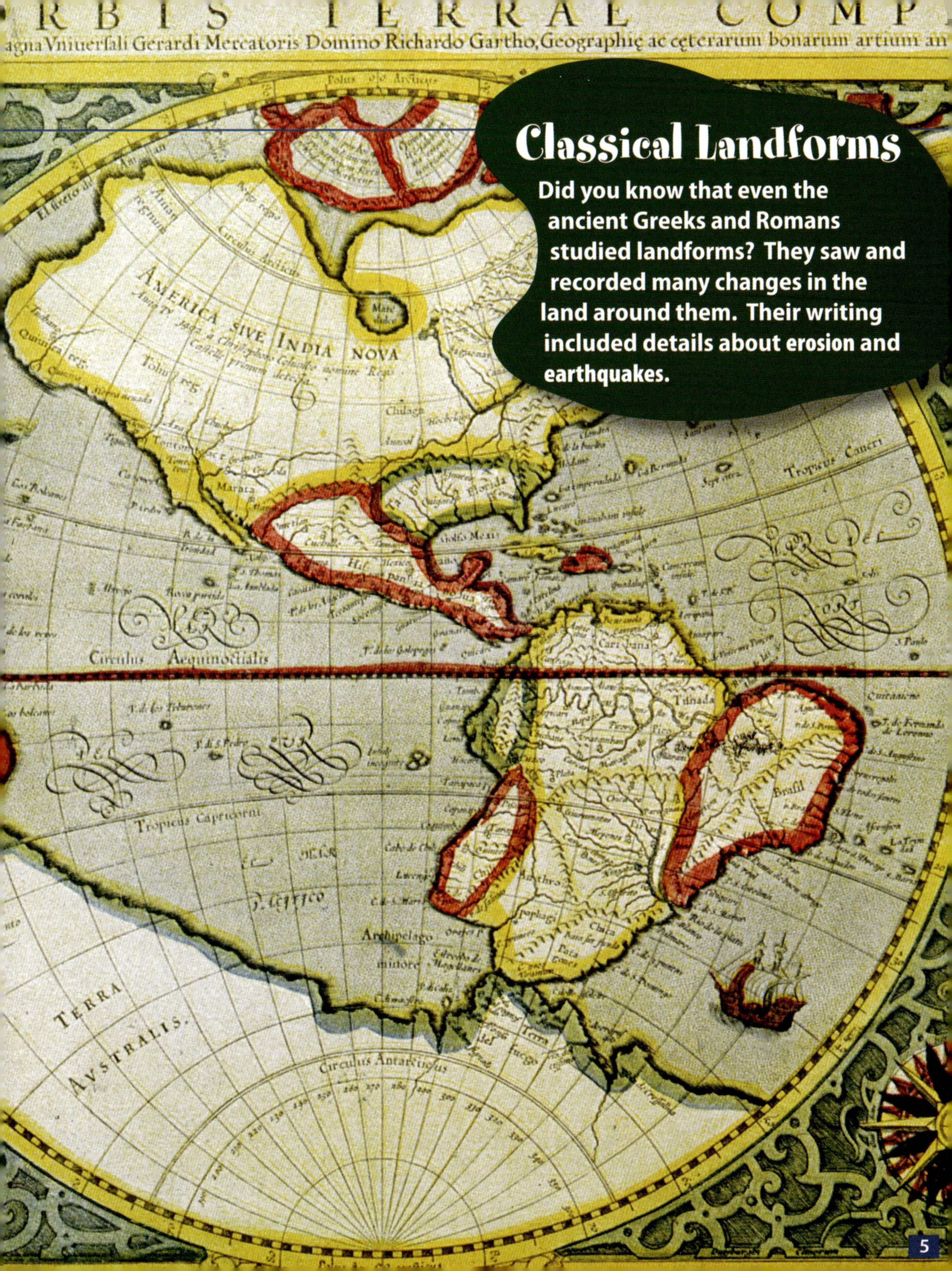

Classical Landforms

Did you know that even the ancient Greeks and Romans studied landforms? They saw and recorded many changes in the land around them. Their writing included details about erosion and earthquakes.

Ellen Churchill Semple
[1863–1932]

Ellen Semple was born in Kentucky. She loved to read books about history and travel. When her interest turned to geography, she decided to move to Germany. She lived with a German family so she could learn to speak the language. The problem was that Germany at that time did not allow women to graduate from their schools. So, she just sat in on the classes, learning all she could.

When she returned to America, she continued studying on her own. She went on to teach at the University of Chicago. She translated the work of German geographers into English. She wrote her own books, too. She showed how geography affects how people live. Semple is said to be America's first influential female geographer.

The first globes were made by carving a sphere of wood or brass. This was difficult to do. The globes were made one at a time. Each one took a very long time to finish.

Mercator wanted to make the process easier so that many globes could be made at the same time. He started by making a wooden mold. Then he covered it with **papier mâché.** Next, he glued a printed world map on the form. Caps were placed where the map came together at the poles. Lastly, the globe was hand-painted with watercolors and set in a wooden stand. Today most globes are made by machine, using the same basic idea.

Maps and globes are important and useful for many reasons. Perhaps they are most useful to the scientists who study the earth. They show the lay of the land. And they guide people where they want to go.

This book is something like a map. It will take you on a journey to the lives and work of some of history's most important earth scientists.

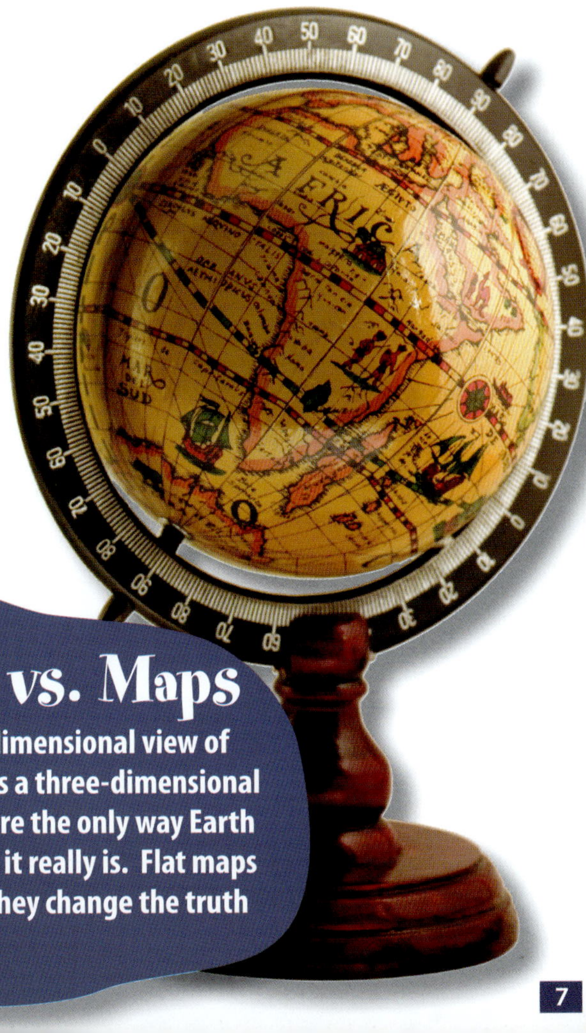

Globes vs. Maps

A map is a two-dimensional view of Earth. A globe is a three-dimensional model. Globes are the only way Earth can be shown as it really is. Flat maps are useful, but they change the truth a little.

Making the Way

People have always wanted to explore the earth. Some of them want to learn about the earth, too. They want to know what it is made of and how it came to be. They are called **geologists**. They are scientists who study the earth and its history.

On the next pages, you will learn about some of the first geologists of modern times.

the Grand Canyon

John Wesley Powell [1834–1902]

John Powell was born in New York. As a child, he liked to go on trips to explore and collect. When he was twenty, he spent four months walking across Wisconsin. He studied wildlife and landforms there. He rowed down the Mississippi and other rivers. He lost one of his arms when he was a soldier during the Civil War. Later, he became a geologist and an explorer of the American West.

Powell loved exploring. He wanted to explore the Grand Canyon. Everyone thought it was impossible. In 1869, Powell gathered nine men, four boats, and enough food for ten months. He didn't know how long the trip would take. They rode rough rapids. Some of their boats turned over. They lost food. Four men left the group. But Powell believed they could make it. And they did! They made it down the Colorado River and through the Grand Canyon. The trip took them three months.

Powell studied the Grand Canyon on the trip. He thought about what he saw. He believed erosion from the Colorado River formed the canyon. His trip proved him right. A couple of years later, he made the trip again. He produced a map of the area.

Powell helped set up the United States Geological Survey (USGS) in 1879. It is an important group of earth scientists. The scientists study land changes. They also study the link between people and the land. This study helps people make important decisions about the earth.

Powell worked with the Paiute Indian tribe on his expedition.

Grove Karl Gilbert [1843–1918]

Grove Karl Gilbert did not plan to be a geologist. He studied Greek and math and became a teacher. He soon realized it wasn't the right job for him. He started to work at a science center. He studied fossils, rocks, and minerals. On one job, he dug up the bones of an ancient animal. He then learned something about himself. He was more interested in the hole that the bones came from than the bones themselves. He wanted to study how the land was formed and how it changed.

In 1899, Gilbert was picked to go on a trip along the coast of Alaska. A rich railroad builder took 126 scientists and artists on the trip. The trip was the largest and most well known that the world had ever seen. Gilbert went on the trip to study **glaciers** and **landforms**. He took many photographs and wrote a book about them. Many people thought it was the best book from the trip.

In 1905, Gilbert went to California to study gold mining. He always wanted to feel an **earthquake**, and in 1906 he got his wish. The great San Francisco earthquake hit. He felt its power, and he saw its destruction. Gilbert spent months studying the damage and causes of the disaster.

Grove Karl Gilbert

A huge wave churning the sand can do great damage.

Earthquakes Under the Ocean

A terrible 2004 earthquake in the Indian Ocean started deadly **tsunamis**. The waves killed more than 200,000 people. The size of the earthquake was between 9.1 and 9.3. It was the fourth-largest one ever recorded. It was large enough to vibrate the entire planet at least half an inch. It set off earthquakes in other places, too. Scientists are studying the data from many **seismographs** to learn more about this earthquake. They hope what they learn will help to predict future earthquakes.

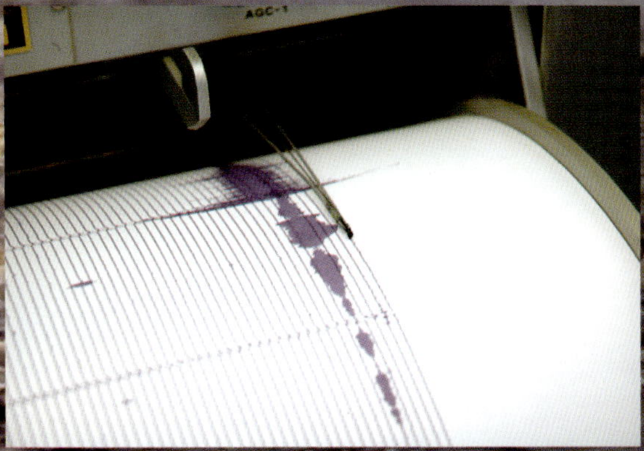

A seismograph shows and records the power of earthquakes.

William Morris Davis (1850–1934)

William Davis was born in the United States. His mother and grandmother raised him. His father was away in the Civil War.

As a boy, Davis was curious about the world around him. He wanted to explore. So, as an adult, he went to South America. He worked for three years at an **observatory** there. An observatory is used to study space. When Davis came home, he studied geology and geography. Geography hadn't been widely studied up until that time. Davis wanted to change that. He thought everyone should know about the places on our planet.

Davis helped make geography a school subject. He wanted students to know more than the names of places and where

Modern technology in today's observatories allows us to see even farther and more clearly into the heavens.

This is a sample of a block diagram. It shows the area beneath the surface of the land.

they are found. He wanted them to study landforms. He thought they should know what makes and changes the earth. Davis is called the founder of American geography. He is also known as a founder of **geomorphology**. That is the study of landforms.

Davis changed geography for scientists, too. He helped them learn a new way to look at and record their research. He told them to use maps and **block diagrams.** Block diagrams show a piece of something as if it had been cut like a slice of cake. They show what we can't see on the surface. For example, they can show the layers of soil and rock in a hillside.

Be a Modern-Day Explorer

Explorers of old crossed unknown lands to learn what was out there. Would you like to be a modern-day explorer? How about hitching a ride to the International Space Station? When finished, it will be the largest orbiting spacecraft in history. Scientists can study Earth's landforms there. Maybe you would rather explore under the sea. You can use the Aquarius Undersea Laboratory to study landforms there. It's the only research lab under the water. Scientists live and work there with all the comforts of a modern lab. So, where will you go?

In the 1870s, people did not understand how landforms were created. They didn't know how they changed over time. In fact, many people believed that the Bible's great flood made all the landforms.

Davis wanted to learn more. He began studying landforms. He described how landforms are created. Rivers can change the landscape to make new landforms. He called this process the **cycle of erosion.** Geologists today know that the cycle of erosion has a lot to do with Earth's changing surface.

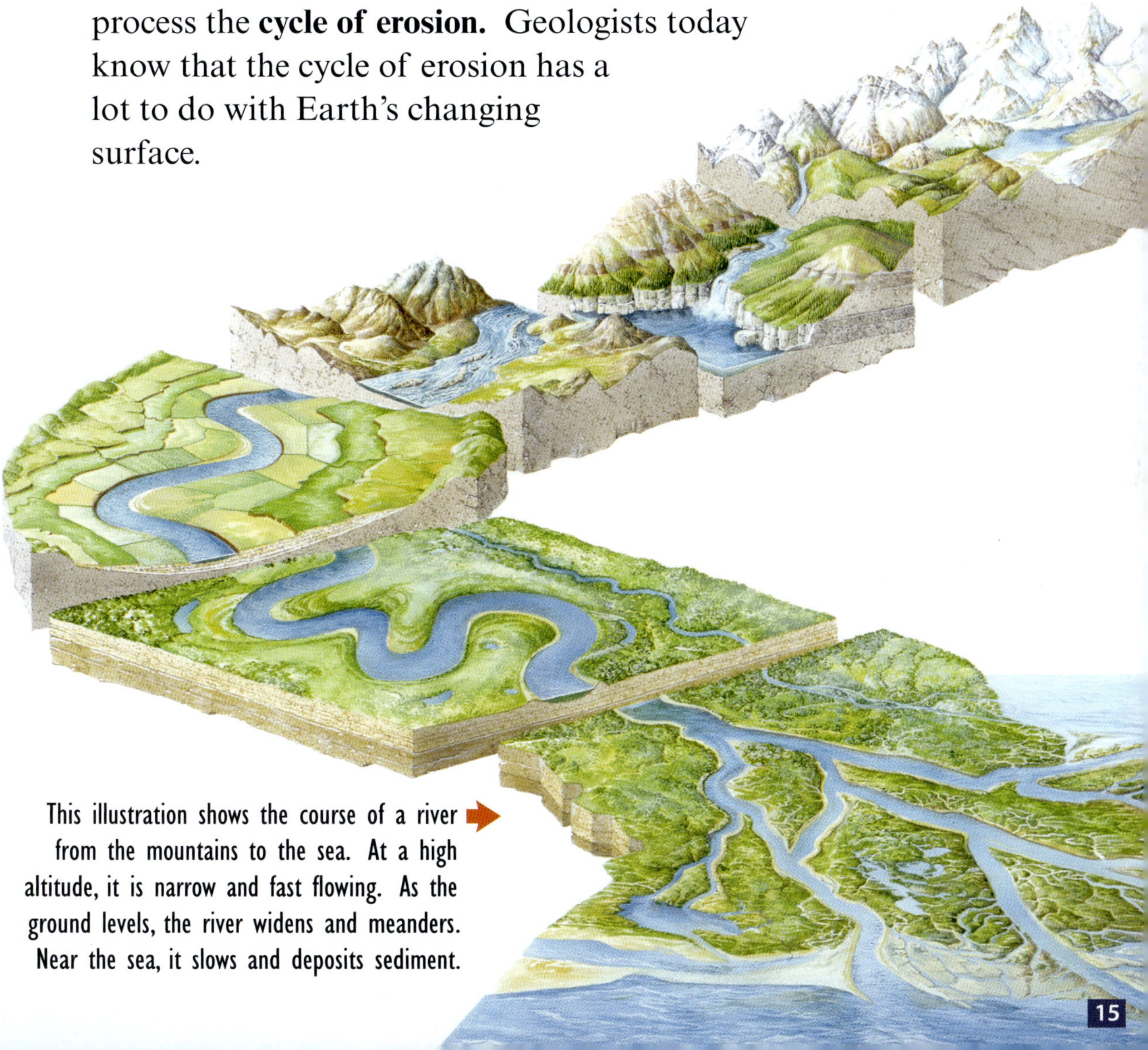

This illustration shows the course of a river from the mountains to the sea. At a high altitude, it is narrow and fast flowing. As the ground levels, the river widens and meanders. Near the sea, it slows and deposits sediment.

Davis' Cycle of Erosion

The cycle of erosion that Davis described has three time periods. They are *youth*, *maturity*, and *old age*. When mountains are first formed, they are young. They are high and have a jagged surface. Then, flowing water begins to create a V-shaped valley.

Over time, the flowing water makes the valley wider. That is erosion caused by water. This is called maturity.

In time, the mountains become gently rolling hills. Erosion caused by time, wear, wind, and water makes this happen. This is called old age.

Two more processes were later added to Davis' cycle. They are called **base level** and **rejuvenation**. Some mountains wear down until all that is left is a flat, level plain. When this reaches sea level, it is called the base level. Volcanoes and earthquakes can create new mountains. When more mountains are created, the cycle starts again. This is called rejuvenation.

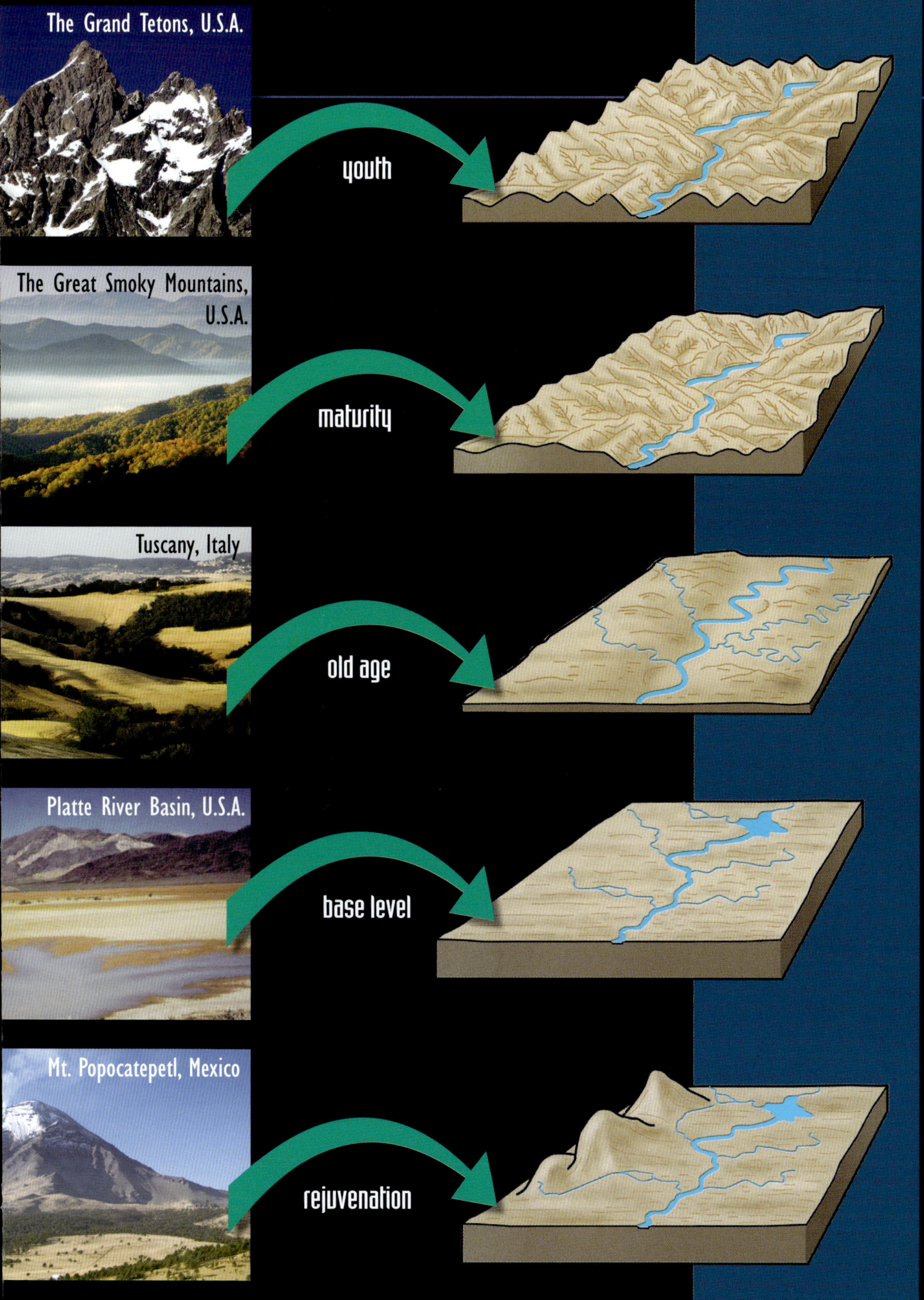
The Grand Tetons, U.S.A.
youth
The Great Smoky Mountains, U.S.A.
maturity
Tuscany, Italy
old age
Platte River Basin, U.S.A.
base level
Mt. Popocatepetl, Mexico
rejuvenation

Changing the Map

Earth scientists continued to study the earth. But one person thought he could do a better job. He especially thought the maps being made and used could be better. That person was Albrecht Penck.

Albrecht Penck [1858–1945]

Penck was a German geographer and geologist. He was a science professor for many years. He is well known for his study of glaciers and their effects.

There are two main types of glaciers. Valley or mountain glaciers move down from the mountaintops into the valleys between the mountains. **Gravity** makes them move.

Albrecht Penck

Continental glaciers are the glaciers from the **ice ages.** They cover large areas of the earth. Glaciers change landforms in a big way. Today, the only continental glaciers cover much of Greenland and Antarctica.

The study of glaciers is important. But Penck may be even more known for the way he improved maps.

continental glacier in Greenland

mountain glacier in Canada

Florence Bascom

[1862–1945]

Florence Bascom was born in Massachusetts. As a child, she would go on drives with her father and his friend. His friend was a geology teacher. Bascom became interested in geology. Bascom was one of the first female geologists in the United States. She was the second woman to earn a Ph.D. (the highest degree possible) in geology in the country. While she was going to school, she had to sit behind a screen. Women were not yet allowed in the school, and they did not want her to distract the men. Among other things, she studied rocks and how mountains were formed. She used her knowledge of rocks to learn how the Appalachian Mountains were formed. Other scientists think she is one of the country's most important geologists.

The Millionth Map of the World Project

Albrecht Penck was not happy about the maps that were being made. Everyone used a different style and scale. It was hard to compare one map with another. He thought map making should follow set rules. He wanted maps to have a scale of one-to-one-million (1 cm = 10 km or 1 inch = 15.8 miles).

Penck suggested this idea to scientists of the world. Many thought it was a good idea. In 1913, they began a project called the Millionth Map of the World. It was named this

because it used the one-to-one-millionth scale. The group also decided to use the Roman alphabet for all maps. This meant that countries with other alphabets would need to translate them into the Roman alphabet. (Of course, then they couldn't be easily read in their own countries!) They also agreed on standard colors. Towns, railroads, and boundaries would be in black. Roads would be red. Land features would be brown.

Each country was supposed to create its own map. This caused many problems. Not every country could afford to do so, or had mapmakers who could do it. It also took some countries longer to finish than others. Some maps were outdated by the time others were made. In the end, only about one-third of the maps of the countries were made.

Even though it failed, many people thought that Penck's idea had merit. Others did not agree. Given what you know, was the Millionth Map project a worthwhile one?

No Date

As a rule, many mapmakers don't date their maps or globes. Perhaps they don't want the maps to seem outdated, even when they are.

Protecting Nature's Beauty

For many years, people enjoyed the beauty of the wild and natural lands all around them. As more people were born, people began to use more industry. More people and more industry meant trouble for the land. Earth scientists knew they had to protect the land for the future. Scientists such as John Muir studied the land and nature. These scientists began to work to preserve it. They wanted it to be there always.

Today, many countries have **national parks.** The parks protect special landforms for people to enjoy in the future. They keep the land from being damaged or changed by people.

John Muir

Ayers Rock, Australia

On the next two pages is a list of some of the world's protected landforms.

- Lake Louise and Lake Moraine in Canada have mountain glaciers in them.
- Ayers Rock in Australia is the world's largest **monolith**. It is a sacred site for the native people. It is also one of Australia's most famous natural landmarks.

World Heritage Sites

The United Nations Educational, Scientific, and Cultural Organization (UNESCO) protects many landforms around the world. There are more than 800 sites on the **World Heritage List.**

Lake Louise in Alberta, Canada

Mt. Fuji, Japan

Galapagos Islands

Machu Picchu, Peru

Great Barrier Reef, Australia

Carlsbad Caverns, New Mexico

- Mt. Fuji in Japan is one of the most familiar mountains in the world. It is Japan's highest mountain. It is also an active **volcano**.
- The Galapagos Islands are located off the coast of Ecuador. There are six large islands and several smaller islands. Volcanoes formed these islands. Some of the volcanoes are still active.
- Machu Picchu in Peru is one of the world's most amazing ruins. It has been called the "Lost City of the Incas." This ancient city is high in the Andes Mountains.
- The Great Barrier Reef in Australia has more than 2,800 beautiful coral reefs. The reefs are being damaged from human use. Scientists are working hard to protect them.
- Carlsbad Caverns in New Mexico has more than 80 amazing caves. They have spectacular mineral formations.

Rachel Louise Carson

(1907–1964)

Rachel Carson was raised on a farm in Pennsylvania. As a little girl, she dreamed of being a writer. She published her first story when she was only 10 years old! She also had a love of nature, which she shared with her mother. Carson went to college, earning a degree in zoology. That is the science of animal life. She was hired to write scripts for radio shows. To add to her income, she began to write about science. She wrote about the beauty and wonder of the ocean. She encouraged others to appreciate and enjoy them. She became well known in the 1960s when she wrote a book called *Silent Spring.* The book is about the effects of **pesticides** on the environment. She did a lot of work with the Environmental Protection Agency. She was most influential in getting the environmentalist movement going.

Geologist: Diane Evans

Jet Propulsion Laboratory

"I started out trying to learn how to study Mars' rocks from space. Then I thought, 'Why don't we do this using the same technique on Earth?'"

Cool View

How do you explore our planet? Do you look at rocks up close? Have you seen your town from a tall building? Diane Evans has a very different view. She explores Earth from space.

Satellites orbit our planet from hundreds of miles up and beam down information. "Satellites give a wide view, so you can see patterns," Evans tells Sally Ride Science. From a satellite photograph, she can watch for things like giant cracks in the ground. These could be a sign of earthquake danger.

She can also see patterns in the ocean. These might tell her about changes in climate. Satellites even "see" things that are normally invisible, such as the temperature of the ocean. They can measure how deep the ocean is.

Evans has traveled all over the world examining Earth up close. But there's no place like space for a cool view.

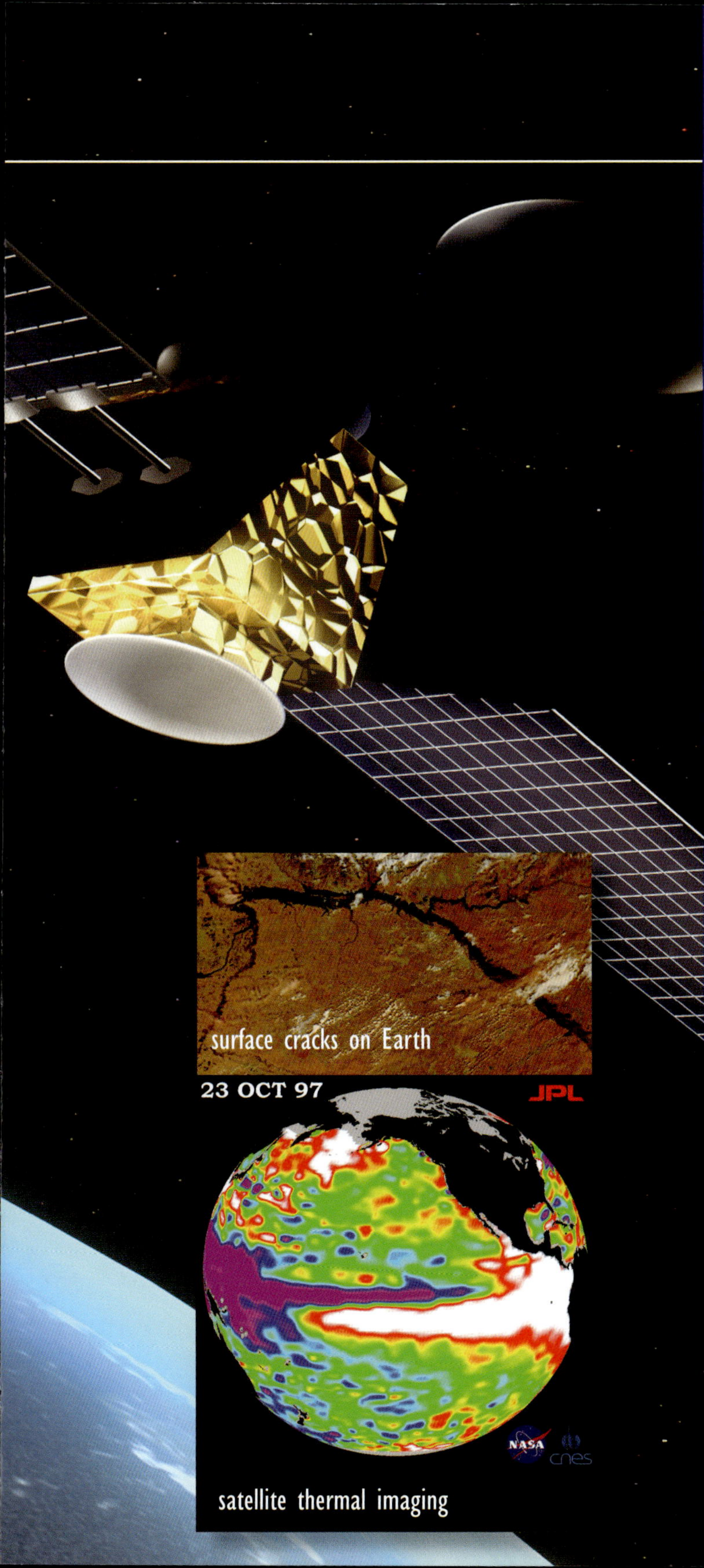

surface cracks on Earth

satellite thermal imaging

Being There

If you were a geologist, you would study Earth's rock and soil. Some other jobs you could have are...

- Looking for underground mineral deposits.
- Learning how to clean up contaminated soil.
- Studying how to prevent landslides.

For You to Do

If you flew high above your town, what patterns or shapes do you think you might see? Think about roads, rivers, and parks.

Did You Know?

What exactly is a satellite? It's something that orbits Earth. Human-made satellites come in all sizes. They are powered by solar panels that stick out like wings. A big satellite might be about the size of a school bus.

Lab: Earth Movement

This lab will explore the effects of rainfall on the movement of earth down a slope.

Materials

- soil
- sand
- gravel
- large tray with edges
- water
- watering can

Procedure

1. Build a model mountain on the tray with the gravel, sand, and soil.
2. Use the watering can to sprinkle water on the mountain. What does this simulate? (light rain)
3. Increase the water flow on the mountain to a pour. What does this simulate? (heavy rain)
4. Record what you see. What type of movement took place (landslide, mudslide, or slump)? Was the movement different depending on the flow of the water? If yes, in what way?
5. What type of force is responsible for this type of movement? (gravity)

Extension Idea for Further Study

- Create different landforms like hills, valleys, and plains.
- Test the effects of different forces such as wind.

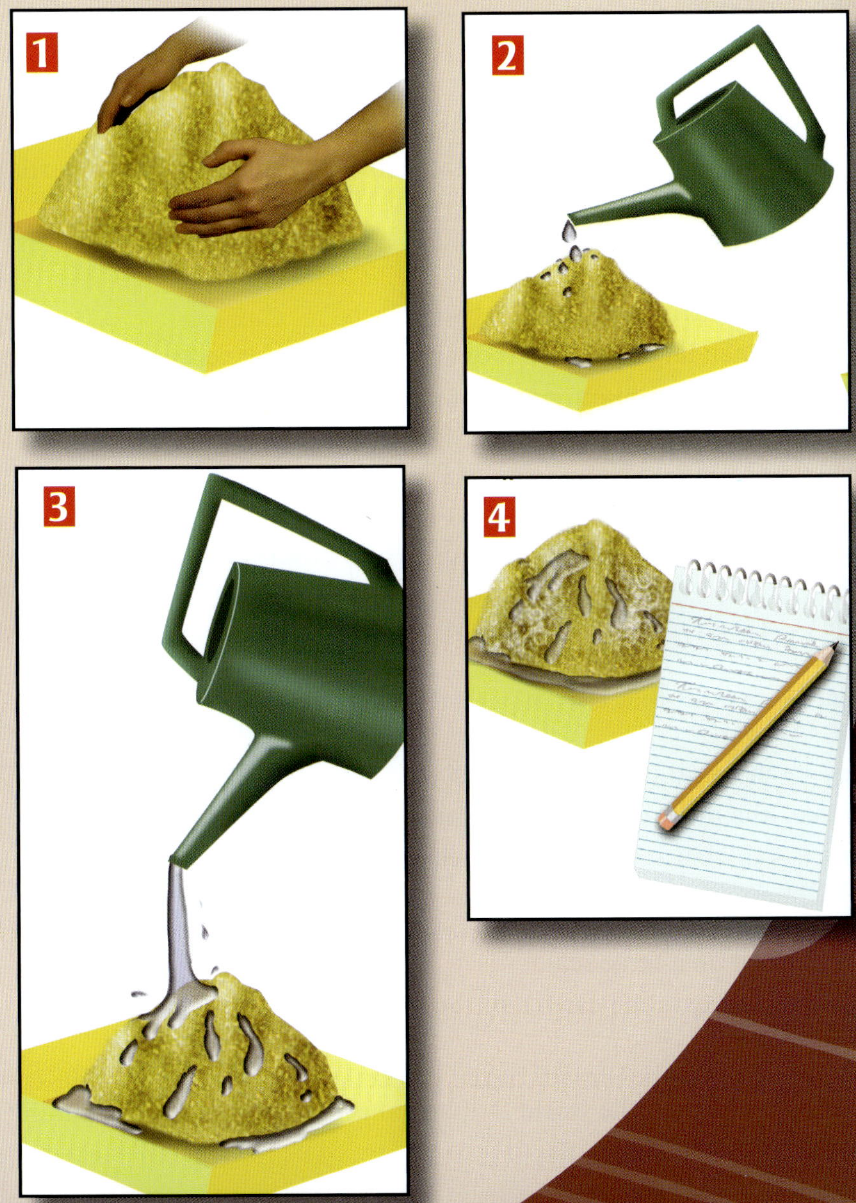

Glossary

base level—lowest level that water can erode a landform; sea level

block diagram—three-dimensional cutaway diagram

cycle of erosion—model for stream erosion proposed by William Morris Davis in the late 1800s

earthquake—a violent shaking of the earth's crust to release stress along a fault line

erosion—gradual wearing away of rock or soil

geography—the study of the earth and its features

geologist—someone who studies rocks and minerals and the structure of the earth

geomorphology—the study of landforms

glacier—a large body of ice and snow that either doesn't melt or just partially melts in the summer

globe—a sphere that represents the earth or a planet that shows landforms, water, and countries

gravity—force of attraction between two objects

ice age—time when large areas of the earth's surface were covered with glaciers

landform—a valley, mountain, or plain; parts of the earth's surface

map projection—a way to display the information from a three-dimensional globe to a flat map

monolith—a tall block of solid stone standing by itself

national parks—a large area of land chosen by a government and given special protection

observatory—a building from which scientists can watch the stars, the planets, the weather, etc.

papier mâché—a craft that uses paper and paste to cover a frame and make a model

pesticides—a chemical used to kill pests

rejuvenation—the process of new mountains forming at base level

seismograph—an instrument used to measure and record motions of the earth called seismic waves

tsunami—a single wave or series of waves generated when a body of water is quickly displaced on a large scale

volcano—an opening in the earth's surface through which molten, gaseous, and solid material escape

World Heritage List—the identification, protection, and preservation of cultural and natural sites around the world that are considered to be of outstanding value to humanity

Index

Aquarius Undersea Laboratory, 14
Ayers Rock, 22–23
Bascom, Florence, 19
base level, 16–17
block diagram, 13
Carlsbad Caverns, 24
Carson, Rachel, 25
continental glaciers, 18
cycle of erosion, 15, 16–17
Davis, William, 12–13, 15, 16
earthquake, 5, 10–11, 26–27
Environmental Protection Agency, 25
erosion, 5, 8–9, 15, 16–17
Evans, Diane, 26–27
Galapagos Islands, 24
geographer, 7, 18
geography, 4–7, 12–13
geologist, 8–10, 15, 18–19, 26–27
geomorphology, 13
Gilbert, Grove Karl, 10
glacier, 10, 18–19, 23
globe, 4–7, 21
gravity, 19, 28–29
Great Barrier Reef, 24
Greeks, 5
ice age, 19
International Space Station, 14
Lake Louise, 23
Lake Moraine, 23
landform, 5, 9–10, 13–15, 19, 22, 28–29
Machu Picchu, 24
map projection, 4–5
maps, 4–6, 9, 13, 18–21
Mercator, Gerardus, 4–6
Millionth Map of the World Project, 20–21
monolith, 23
Mt. Fuji, 24
Muir, John, 22
national parks, 22–23
observatory, 12
Penck, Albrecht, 18–21
pesticide, 25
Powell, John Wesley, 9
rejuvenation, 16–17
Romans, 5
seismograph, 11
Semple, Ellen, 7
tsunami, 11
UNESCO, 23
United States Geological Survey, 9
volcano, 24
World Heritage List, 23

Sally Ride Science

Sally Ride Science™ is an innovative content company dedicated to fueling young people's interests in science. Our publications and programs provide opportunities for students and teachers to explore the captivating world of science—from astrobiology to zoology. We bring science to life and show young people that science is creative, collaborative, fascinating, and fun.

Image Credits

Cover: Jaan-Martin Kuusmann/Shutterstock; p.3 CORBIS; p.4 (top) Steven Wright/Shutterstock; p.4 (right) The Granger Collection, New York; p.4–5 Mary Evans Picture Library/Alamy; p.6 (background) Mary Evans Picture Library/Alamy; p.6 Rick Reason; p.7 Elena Kalistratova/Shutterstock; p.8 (top) Mike Morley/iStockphoto; p.8 Laurin Rinder/Shutterstock; p.8 (right) Smithsonian Institution, Bureau of American Ethnology/USGS; p.9 The Granger Collection, New York; p.10 USGS; p.11 (background) Radu Razvan/Shutterstock; p.11 iStockphoto; p.12 (left) Rob Sylvan/iStockphoto; p.12 (right) SPL/Photo Researchers, Inc.; 13 Tim Bradley; p.14 GARY HINCKS/SCIENCE PHOTO LIBRARY; p.15 NASA; p.16–17 (top to bottom) Sascha Burkard/Shutterstock; Michael Hare/Shutterstock; Iofoto/Shutterstock; dartmouth.edu; Marco Regalia/Shutterstock; p.18 (top) BORTEL Pavel/Shutterstock; p.18 (left) LOC/Photo researchers; p.18–19 (top) Tyler Olson/Shutterstock; p.18–19 (bottom) Jason Cheever/Shutterstock; p.19 (background) BORTEL Pavel/Shutterstock; p.19 USGS; p.20–21 Photos.com; p.22 (top) Michael J Thompson/Shutterstock; p.22 (bottom) North Wind Picture Archives/Alamy; p.22–23 Xufang/Shutterstock; p.23 Goncalo Veloso de Figueiredo/Shutterstock; p.24 (top to bottom) Photos.com; Shutterstock; Dan Cooper/iStockphoto; Ian Scott/Shutterstock; Gary L. Brewer/Shutterstock; p.25 (background) Peter Clark/Shutterstock; p.25 Alfred Eisenstaedt//Time & Life Pictures/Getty Images; p.26–27 Sebastian Kaulitzki/Shutterstock; p.27 (bottom) NASA; p.28 (top) BarbaraJH/Shutterstock; p. 28–29 Nicoll Rager Fuller